Sales Strategy From The Inside Out

How complex selling really works

DUANE SPARKS

The Sales Board, Inc.

The Sales Board, Inc.

14505 21st Ave. N.
Minneapolis, MN 55447
(800) 232-3485
www.TheSalesBoard.com
www.ActionSelling.com

ISBN-10: 10-9753569-1-7
ISBN-13: 978-0-9753569-1-3

Printed in the United States of America

First Printing November 2008

FORWARD

I read "Sales Strategy From The Inside Out" and enjoyed it. Then I went back to highlight key parts. When I was done, I realized that I had highlighted the whole book.

At Sundyne Corp. we sell pumps, compressors and other products to the industrial market. Ninety percent of our sales efforts are "complex," meaning that our field salespeople must call on multiple decision makers at different buying levels at a prospective account. Sometimes the decision makers even work for different organizations, since large companies outsource some of their engineering work to consultants, and we call on the consulting company as well as the end user.

The reason I got so busy with the highlighter is that Duane Sparks has packed his new book with rich insights into the kind of selling we do. Sundyne already uses the *Action Selling* system that works so well for Carrie, Ron, and Darrel, the sellers who speak in these pages. It works extremely well for us, too. But even though I know the system, many insights were fresh to me, or struck with new force.

Perhaps the most fundamental one is this: Regardless of the complexity of the situation, or which decision maker we're dealing with, the sales process is the same. We can use the same 9 Acts with an engineer or a CEO. Talk about a useful strategic roadmap!

Readers familiar with *Action Selling* will know what I mean by "9 Acts." (Those who don't are about to have their eyes opened.) This brings up another point I highlighted: Language matters.

Before Sundyne adopted *Action Selling*, our greatest difficulties in planning effective sales calls came from communication challenges. Now we have a common language to speak with our sales force and channel partners. We used to focus on presenting product features. Now we are focused on "Commitment Objective" and "Asking the Best Questions." In product knowledge training we now emphasize the needs that the product satisfies and what questions to ask to uncover those needs. We break it down by types of decision makers, so we develop questions that we will ask to decision makers with different levels of authority.

Then there's the concept that selling must be a team sport. If you want to drive sales results regardless of the economic environment, then management—not just salespeople—must be educated on *Action Selling* and able to speak the language. I love the peer-to-peer phone calls made in this book. In the future, I'm going to have our VP call the VP of prospective companies just to provide assurance that we are very aware of their needs and that we have our best people working on the project.

Several Sundyne salespeople have said that *Action Selling* changed their lives. This is a book that could change yours.

Alan Brown
Sales Manager, Americas
Sundyne Corp.

Introduction

Wrong strategy? Why didn't you ask?

I n this book you will meet six fictional characters who tell the tale of a business-to-business sales process, each from his or her own point of view. But let me begin with a story that is not fictional but real.

On August 1, 2007, the heavily trafficked I-35W bridge in Minneapolis collapsed and fell into the Mississippi River. When the initial shock of the tragedy wore off, the Minnesota Department of Transportation hurried to replace the bridge. The contract to construct a new one went out to bid.

The business was won by a Colorado outfit, the only bidder that had never built a bridge in Minnesota. Its proposal carried the highest price tag and one of the slowest delivery times. Its local competitors were so outraged that they filed an unsuccessful lawsuit.

How did the out-of-state firm win the $250 million contract? The committee that made the decision explained that price and speed of delivery were not the only criteria it considered. Eight other factors were on the committee's wish list. The competitors cried foul. "You never told us that!" they roared.

"You never asked," the committee replied. "The winning bidder did."

In other words, the outsiders clinched a huge deal for one simple reason: They asked the best questions. The competition assumed they knew what mattered to the buyers, and pitched products accordingly. The Colorado people assumed nothing—except that their job was to find out what mattered and why. The insiders saw the deal as a straight bidding affair. The outsiders recognized the situation for what it was: a complex selling environment.

I love that story because it demonstrates what I believe is a great truth about selling. Real professionals don't sell with great pitches. They sell by asking great questions. The more complex the sales environment—with multiple decision makers and multiple buying criteria—the more important this principle becomes.

Here's another truth. When you ask the best questions and use what you learn to create the best sales strategy, "complex" sales get a lot less complex.

How hard does it have to be?

That is the message I have tried to convey in this book. Complex sales don't have to be complex at all. No matter how many decision makers are in the picture, no matter how many criteria arise, a sale still boils down to fundamentals. Those who ask the best questions earn the right to ask more questions. They discover more relevant information than anyone else. And they sell themselves in the process.

That is always your first major task as a salesperson: to sell yourself. If you can do that, you will find it much easier to fulfill the primary duty of every salesperson, which is to gain commitment from customers.

Commitments must be gained at each step in any sales process, up to and including the final buying decision. A "complex" sale in a business-to-business environment has more steps and more players than a simple person-to-person transaction, but you don't need a whole new set of principles or techniques to gain commitment at each step. The same behaviors that persuaded Decision Maker A to take the previous step will persuade Decision Makers B, C, and D to take the next ones.

Process produces strategy

But what should the next step be? That's where salespeople lose their way in business-to-business selling situations, because very few are really good at sales strategy. Most understand product features and benefits. Some understand how their products serve clients' business needs. But only a handful grasp the real reason why people buy in a complex sale: because their personal needs are met.

A sales strategy that is not based on uncovering and serving the personal needs of the buyers involved is doomed. And when I say buyers, I mean all of them. If your so-called strategy for a complex sale is to brush aside lower-level "influencers" and fight your way straight to the ultimate decision maker, you are going to lose a lot more deals than you win.

When it comes to strategy, what most salespeople lack is a comprehensive process—a system—that provides a reliable way to 1) gather information, 2) uncover buyers' business and personal needs in a way that builds trust, 3) use the information to determine the next logical step on the path toward a sale and, 4) use the trust to gain each buyer's commitment to take that step.

Easy to say, but how does it work? What does it look like and feel like when sellers employ such a process in a complex sales environment? I have seen it many times. This book is my attempt to capture and describe it, from both the buyers' and sellers' points of view.

Like my four previous books, this one tells a story. But it does so in a different form. You will hear from three decision makers at a fictional organization called Amstand Corp. and from three players at GoTeam Unlimited, a company that would like very much to make a major sale to Amstand.

What the sellers do

The system that these sellers employ—and to which the buyers react—is Action Selling. I humbly submit (all right, not so humbly) that Action Selling provides the best available means both to devise an effective strategy for a complex sale and to execute that strategy successfully.

In my earlier books, the Action Selling system is described in some detail. That is not my purpose here. On pages X & XI, immediately following this introduction, you will find a bare-bones explanation of the system's basic elements and vocabulary: its 9 Acts and the 5 Buying Decisions that the Acts are designed to target. Our three fictional sellers will use some of that vocabulary, and readers unfamiliar with the system will find it helpful to see how the pieces fit together.

But my goal in this book is not to explain the system. Instead I have tried to get inside the heads of the people involved in the transaction to show how and why a genuinely strategic sales approach works. After all, it is inside the buyers' heads that any sales approach succeeds or fails.

Let me say this, however, about the framework that guides the sellers' activities. Action Selling is not something I made up one day out of thin air. Here's a bit of history.

Since the need for a "sales force" first arose during the Industrial Revolution of the 19th Century, a great many thinkers have tried to figure out the best ways to sell—and to teach people how to sell effectively. I researched more than 500 books on the sales process before I devised Action Selling.

The 5 Buying Decisions that every customer makes? They were identified in 1936 by Burton Bigelow in his book "The Knack of Selling More." But Bigelow had them out of sequence (his order: Brand, Price, Firm, Salesperson, Time). That error was corrected in 1953 by R.W. Husband in "The Psychology of Successful Selling." R.W got it right: Salesperson, Company, Product, Price, Time to Buy.

The 9 Acts of Action Selling? In 1898, E. St. Elmo Lewis formulated the idea that the sales process can and should be broken into discrete steps. He was onto something, but he focused on the "pitch," a word that I hate almost as much as I hate the idea it implies: that selling is mostly about talking, rather than listening.

The emphasis on identifying and then satisfying customer needs, which is the heart and soul of Action Selling? Need Satisfaction Theory, the fundamental basis of all "consultative selling" approaches, was formulated in 1915 by Tipper, Hollingsworth, Hotchkiss, and Parsons. (It took four guys to figure this out back then.)

I tell you all of that only to assure you that the system I am recommending has its roots in a considerable body of thought and research. Knowing the history will not help you sell more effectively in a complex, business-to-business environment. But if I have achieved my goal, reading this book will.

Duane Sparks
Chairman, The Sales Board
Author of Action Selling

ACTION SELLING IN BRIEF

The 5 Buying Decisions

Action Selling is built upon this research-proven fact: A customer's "buying decision" is not really singular but plural. In choosing whether to purchase something from a salesperson, customers actually make five major buying decisions. What's more—this is crucial—they always make those decisions in the same order. And no, price is not number one.

1. Salesperson
You can't sell a product before you sell yourself. Unless customers first decide to buy you, the salesperson, they will not buy anything from you. The decision hinges on whether they find you likeable, honest, credible, and, above all, trustworthy. Selling yourself first is so crucial that the first four Acts of Action Selling are devoted to it.

2. Company
In deciding whether to "buy" the salesperson's company, the customer weighs matters including its reputation, expertise, policies, and whether it is a good match for the customer's company.

3. Product
Which of the customer's needs will the product address? Will it solve important problems? Create opportunities? Does its quality stack up well against the competition?

4. Price
Is the solution worth the cost? Is it a good value compared with competitive offerings?

5. Time to Buy
When does the customer need the results that the product will deliver? How soon must he make up his mind?

A sale is made *only* when the customer makes the first four decisions in your favor and determines that the time to buy is now. If any of these decisions go against you, the sale is lost.

The 9 Acts

Though they usually aren't aware of it, customers always make the 5 Buying Decisions in the same order. The 9 Acts of Action Selling are designed and arranged to keep the sales process moving forward by maximizing the odds that the customer will make each decision in your favor. Together, the Acts comprise a step-by-step strategy for successful sales calls.

Act 1: Commitment Objective
The salesperson must have a preplanned Commitment Objective for every sales call. This is a goal to gain the customer's agreement to take the next logical step toward a final buying decision. What must the customer agree to *do* that will keep the process moving forward?

Act 2: People Skills
Open the call by using interpersonal skills to establish rapport with the customer and begin to build a trusting relationship. The single most important "people skill" is effective listening.

Act 3: Ask the Best Questions
Uncover needs and continue to build trust by asking thoughtful questions about problems and opportunities facing the customer's company and the customer personally. How does the company win or lose in its business? What would a personal win for this customer look like? What other decision makers have a stake in the situation?

Act 4: Agree on Need
Ensure that you have understood the customer's answers to your questions and gain explicit agreement that you have identified the customer's most important business and personal needs.

Act 5: Sell the Company
Using what you now know about what really matters to the customer, target those needs directly in explaining why your company would be a good partner to address them.

Act 6: Sell the Product
Present your product or solution, focusing again on its specific application to the customer's agreed-upon needs.

Act 7: Ask for Commitment
Ask the customer to take the step you identified as your Commitment Objective: buy the product, schedule a meeting with other decision makers, etc. Keep the sales process moving.

Act 8: Confirm the Sale
Assure the customer that he has made the right decision, tell him you appreciate the business, and schedule the next event. Take these steps to ward off buyer's remorse.

Act 9: Replay the Call
After every sales call, review your execution of the first eight Acts. What could you do better next time? Perform Act 9 faithfully, and you will never stop improving.

CONTENTS

PREFACE

Strategy is not a knack

I n my 37 years as a salesperson, sales executive and sales trainer, I have known thousands of wonderful salespeople. But in all that time I have met only a handful whom I would consider naturally excellent at sales strategy. I can literally count them on one hand.

When I say "excellent at strategy," I mean salespeople who could think through a complex deal and maintain a clear vision of how and why the deal would happen. Thanks to what I can only call an innate ability, these five individuals could figure out the power relationships in client organizations—which people had the influence, authority, and respect necessary to move the deal forward—and determine the necessary steps to bring those people onboard.

Above all, they were perceptive about the motives of buyers and influencers at various levels and knew what they had to do to help the buyers get what they wanted.

No, they weren't clairvoyant. Their abilities had to do with asking great questions and thereby earning the right to ask more great questions. They wound up knowing who was who, and what was what, and how various buyers stood to benefit from the deal because the buyers told them. The buyers told them because great questions build trust, and trust creates allies.

Those five people were naturals. Every other salesperson I've ever known had to be thoroughly trained to reach a comparable level of effectiveness.

A number of books have been written on sales strategy. Some of them are very good. A few years ago I met Steve Heiman, author of the great book, "Strategic Selling." I hold his work in very high regard. He documents, in great detail, the different types of buyers that exist in organizations and how to approach them.

What's lacking even in Heiman's first-rate book, however, is a vivid sense of how salespeople who really "get" strategy actually operate, and why buyers respond to them.

This book is my attempt to fill that gap. I wanted to get inside the heads of some sellers who excel at strategy, and let them describe why and how they do what they do. Likewise, I wanted to get inside the heads of some buyers at different levels in an organization and let those buyers describe what it is about these particular salespeople that makes them stand out from the crowd. Why do the buyers find themselves wanting to do business with these folks and not somebody else?

A complex sale can involve any number of players in the buying and selling companies, but I think that three voices from each side of the fence are enough to illustrate how and why a great sales strategy works. You're going to hear from three people at GoTeam Unlimited, a team of sellers, and from their counterparts in the corporate hierarchy at a client organization called Amstand Companies.

To imagine these characters as fully as possible, I made each of them a composite of some real people I have known. I want to make it clear, however, that no character is based on a single person, and no character is intended to represent any actual person, living or dead.

It is for the reader to judge how realistic I was able to make my characters seem. But I'd like to point out that one of them, at least, is deliberately imperfect. Carrie Overton, the GoTeam salesperson who makes the initial contact at Amstand, is not the most adorable or charismatic or customer-loving person you will ever meet.

This is because she doesn't have to be. One lesson I hope you will take away from this book: Great strategy, and the learnable skills necessary to execute it, do not depend on any special, innate charisma of the salesperson. They depend instead on employing a systematic approach to the sales process that enables people who aren't "naturals"—practically all of us, in other words—to do what the handful of naturals are able to do.

The system that GoTeam uses is Action Selling. The three sellers will describe some of its workings explicitly. But the whole point of using these characters is to let them show you, rather than just tell you, how and why the system works in a complex selling situation.

I am a teacher and trainer at heart, however, so please allow me to spell out a few other lessons that I'm trying to illustrate.

- The GoTeam sellers are great at strategy not individually but in combination. They consult with one another about the Amstand account. They *talk*. It's part of what Action Selling calls "leveraging your resources." If I could find only five naturally great sales strategists in 37 years, maybe we need to put our heads together more often. (Selling happens to be more fun that way, too.)

- Other writers, including Steve Heiman, have suggested that salespeople find a "coach" in the client organization to help them navigate through a complex sale. Basically, the coach is someone to whom you can ask questions such as, "How does the decision process work in your company?" Or, "Who should I speak to about this topic?" I think the idea is great as far as it goes, but why make just one person a coach? Why not learn how to ask great questions and earn the right to ask more questions of every single decision-maker you call upon? Make them all coaches. Once you do, they will gladly give you the information you need to win.

- A related lesson: Lower-level "influencers" are not obstacles to avoid in your quest to get to the person who makes the ultimate buying decision. They are potential allies—every one of them. They should want to take you to the ultimate buyer. Too many salespeople think they're being "strategic" when they find a way over, around, or through a department head, say, to get to a senior executive. When the exec listens to their pitch for five or 10 minutes and then gives them the heave-ho, they think: "Well, at least my strategy worked. I got to the top decision-maker." This is so tragic that I don't know whether to laugh or cry.

I explained in the Introduction that Action Selling is structured upon certain documented knowledge about every buyer's decision-making process (the 5 Buying Decisions). The first of those decisions ("Do I buy the salesperson?") is absolutely critical. As you read what our characters have to say, please notice how everything else flows from that first decision.

Once a decision-maker at any level "buys" the salesperson, he or she begins looking for reasons to buy the product, instead of reasons not to buy. The salesperson gains an ally who provides vital "coaching" information about how to travel the path toward a sale. In a complex sales environment, how do you know what your next step or milestone should be? How do you get the information necessary to achieve that milestone? It all comes from people who have "bought you."

This isn't to say that salespeople don't need to do any homework on their own. It's important to research a client company, and you'll find that lesson embedded in the book too. But if the client company is a maze, it's the buyers' maze. When they, themselves, are leading you through it, a complex sale isn't complex at all.

All 5 Buying Decisions are important. They all matter. But how crucial do I consider the first one: whether to buy the salesperson? You will discover that all of the characters in this book are speaking before GoTeam has presented its product—its proposed solution for Amstand's needs. The issue of price has not yet come up. The first buyer you meet, a middle manager named Nancy Winslow, is going to marvel that "GoTeam still hasn't tried to sell us a solitary thing."

I would argue that Nancy is dead wrong. I think that GoTeam already has sold her the most important thing. I'll leave it to you to decide whether you think GoTeam is going to make a lot of money.

Duane Sparks

Chapter 1

NOT YOUR TYPICAL SALES PITCH

Nancy Winslow

Sales Support Manager

Amstand Companies

Well, nuts. I haven't felt this conflicted since I gave birth to the twins. It should have been my deal—my chance to look like a star. Now it's Victor's deal. Victor Herstad, that is, Amstand's new vice president of business development. . Once I brought him in, he grabbed it like a drowning man clutching a life preserver. And he hasn't let go.

Still, I don't see what I could have done any differently. It isn't as if Victor snuck in and stole the process from me. I had to escalate it to him. There were just too many questions I couldn't answer. Besides, what would a starring role really have gotten me besides a nice pat on the back? A big promotion? To a job with 80-hour weeks, constant travel, and worse headaches than I have now? I'd take a VP's money, but a VP's life—or lack of a life? No thanks. I'll stick with having kids who recognize me.

Like I said, I'm conflicted.

I guess I should back up. This all started when I agreed to meet with Carrie Overton. She's the new sales rep for GoTeam Unlimited, one of our suppliers. As manager of sales support for Amstand Companies, I see quite a few reps who want to sell us everything from training programs and recruitment services to customer relationship management software—CRM systems, if you know the lingo.

I was pretty frazzled when Carrie arrived for the appointment. I was fighting two sudden brush fires—the kind that always break out when I schedule anything, following the universal law that every meeting should occur at the worst possible time.

We had done a little business with GoTeam over the years. To me they were just another specialized vendor. I had met a few times with their previous rep, but I'd have needed to dig out his card to remember his name. A classic pitchman: great buddy on a golf course, no doubt, but essentially a talking sales brochure. Carrie Overton, as far as I knew, would be more of the same, a female version of good old what's-his-name. I wanted her to introduce herself, give me a quick pitch for whatever GoTeam was pushing this quarter, and then get out of my hair.

Carrie opened with some personal questions, trying to build rapport with the client, as salespeople generally do. (I ought to know. My job is to support 200 of them out in the field.) We chatted a bit: I've been with Amstand for 12 years; in my current position here at corporate headquarters for the last eight; I have four kids, including twin sons; yes, they're cute—that sort of thing.

She was pretty good at the personal-rapport bit. Maybe a little too much of a Type A personality to be *great* at faking intense personal interest in me, but pretty good. I mean, I don't see Carrie and me as future Best Friends for Life, but I liked her.

She was smart enough to pick up on my impatience with the personal talk, and she moved on. But not, as I expected, to a sales pitch. Instead she began asking about Amstand Companies. So I gave her a quick overview. We're a major North American distribution company, of course, originally known as Amstand Supply. We're the leader in our industry, with a 25 percent market share. We're successful, our stock is doing pretty well in a tough market, God is in His heaven, all's right with the world.

> *'...she moved on. But not, as I expected, to a sales pitch. Instead she began asking...'*

I looked at my watch. "So what do you have for me today?" I asked, cuing her to deliver the pitch already.

That's when she began to surprise me. Ordinarily, there's nothing salespeople love more than that glorious moment when the preliminaries are out of the way and now they get to launch into their well-practiced spiel. But not Carrie Overton.

"I have no idea if we can do *anything* for you, Nancy," she said. "We may be able to offer you a lot, but I don't know enough about your situation yet to waste your time describing solutions to problems that may not exist. Can we talk a little more about Amstand and your role here?"

Carrie obviously had done some homework, and she started asking questions about the company and how we operate. Very good questions. Maybe she had been a wee bit mechanical with the personal stuff, but there was no mistaking her genuine interest in the business side. With a listener who seemed sincerely fascinated by what I do and who took

'...there was no mistaking her genuine interest... a listener who seemed sincere.'

careful notes, I started talking. Pretty soon I stopped worrying so much about those brush fires I had to fight. They could wait.

Prompted by her questions, I explained that our 25 percent market share came in part from some very smart acquisitions we have made over the past several years. But we like to think it's also because of the way we do business.

Amstand has a strong, value-added sales force. That's our biggest differentiator. Our CEO, Stan Hall, introduced the model when he got the top job 20 years ago, and he has stuck with it. Most of our competitors sell through catalogs—or now via the Internet—which means they have lower costs. But as Stan says, we believe that customers want access to flesh-and-blood salespeople who can help them and add real value to what we sell.

Not that I believe 100 percent of our sales reps are any more valuable than most of the ones who call on me, I thought. I kept that reflection to myself.

Carrie recognized that this means it's crucial for us to maintain a

'She asked me more questions... How do we stay ahead of the pack?'

first-rate sales organization. She asked me more questions about how we operate and how we stay ahead of the pack. I said we're constantly looking for ways to improve. Every company says that, of course. But in fact, I explained, Amstand's new VP of business development, Victor Herstad, was promoted three months ago from a field-manager job with a specific mandate to improve the efficiency and effectiveness of our sales process.

That's when I got onto shaky ground. Carrie wanted to know what kinds of initiatives Victor and I were considering. (Clever of her. Not "What's Victor thinking about?" but "What are you and Victor considering, Nancy?") She asked some perceptive and specific questions that I frankly couldn't answer very well. Victor himself told me that CEO Stan had ordered him to improve efficiency and effectiveness—E&E, we call it. But as to just how we might go about it, Victor hadn't figured that out yet. Or if he had, he'd forgotten to send me the memo.

I certainly wasn't about to give Carrie the impression that I might be out of the loop. Under the E&E heading, Victor and I had talked briefly about several issues: best practices, getting new hires up to speed faster, filling vacant territories, reducing sales costs, providing better forecasting and better management information—a gamut of things. I told Carrie we were evaluating a number of factors and mentioned a few, keeping it deliberately abstract.

> *'...she picked the right time to stop drilling down for details.'*

Maybe she sensed that I was getting uncomfortable. At any rate, she picked the right time to stop drilling down for details. She changed the subject and finally gave me a kind of brief pitch. But it was more a pitch for GoTeam itself than for any of its particular products or services.

Mainly she just said that GoTeam had been able to help several companies with issues surrounding E&E. One client she mentioned was featured two months earlier in a major business magazine for a dramatic turnaround in sales; I remembered the article. And she described GoTeam's activities in a way that suggested expertise in a broader range of solutions than I had known they offered. I thought of them as a pretty narrow niche player.

Carrie said she knew I was pressed for time, and she asked me for another meeting. "As I understand it, you're in the early stages of an important initiative at Amstand," she said. She asked to come back next week with her boss, a GoTeam vice president named Ron Jensen, to get a better handle on our needs in order to see whether GoTeam could offer us anything truly valuable.

"Even if nothing else comes of it, I promise you'll be glad you talked to Ron," Carrie said. "You'll never meet anybody who's a better sounding board when you're thinking through complex issues than Ron Jensen."

'I see a lot of salespeople who call themselves consultative, but I could count on one hand the number who behave like plausible consultants.'

Carrie hadn't even tried to sell me a product or service, but she sure sold me Ron. And I was pretty well sold on Carrie herself. I see a lot of salespeople who like to call themselves "consultative," but I could count on one hand the number who behave like plausible consultants—and it wouldn't take all five fingers. Carrie was plausible.

Why not? I thought. Let's have a look at her hotshot vice president. Maybe he'll turn out to be the pitchman who really replaced old what's-his-name, and I'll find out that this tender concern for understanding our needs is baloney. But if GoTeam is for real, I've got a feeling they just might have some answers that could make yours truly a little old corporate hero.

So I agreed to meet with Carrie and Ron the following week.

Ron turned out to be as impressive as advertised. Now this guy is a business consultant. He really wanted to understand our needs on a deep level. Even his interest in my kids seemed genuine, maybe because he has those twin nieces. He and Carrie worked together like an experienced, professional team, in sync and respectful to each other. And they gave me more background on GoTeam, which has some surprising resources behind it.

> *'Ron and Carrie worked together like an experienced, professional team.'*

Mostly, though, they asked questions. "Sales efficiency and effectiveness" sounds impressive enough, but they wanted to know what E&E actually meant. That was great, but it was also a problem—because I didn't know the answers. We touched on the areas I had mentioned earlier to Carrie—new hires, reducing sales costs, better management information, and so on—but E&E is really Victor's responsibility, and I wasn't sure what Victor had in mind.

I remember three terrific questions they asked—questions fundamental to anything we might try to do: How do you currently measure sales efficiency? How do you define an effective sales force? And how will you know when you have achieved the level of effectiveness you want?

Fundamental, but also above my pay grade. I finally admitted as much, more or less. Believe me, I don't make a habit of passing salespeople up the ladder, but I told them that Victor should be part of this conversation. Ron asked if I would set up a meeting. Or, rather, all he actually asked me to do was pave the way for him to call Victor to see if he could arrange a needs-analysis meeting for the four of us—Ron, Carrie, Victor, and me.

I appreciated the fact that Ron wasn't trying to cut me out of the loop, as a lot of salespeople would have, in his rush to get to the "final decision maker." Then again, maybe he knew that if he ticked me off, I could fix it so he'd never get anywhere near an Amstand buyer ever again. That's a mistake a few sales reps have made over the years. Nobody has made it more than once.

> ## 'He knew that if he ticked me off, he'd never get anywhere near an Amstand buyer.'

At any rate, I agreed. After Ron and Carrie left, I told Victor that a GoTeam vice president would phone, and I urged him to take the call. "I think these people may have some good ideas for us on E&E," I said.

Whatever Ron told Victor in that phone call, it worked. When the four of us sat down a week later, Victor was pumped to talk about our needs. In fact, there was a strange undercurrent of urgency to the meeting that I still don't quite get. Amstand is doing just fine, after all. Anything we can do to improve sales E&E is important, naturally, and I realize it's a priority for Victor. But it isn't a life-or-death issue for the company. At least, not as far as I know.

Anyway, Carrie and Ron were as impressive with Victor in the room as they were with me. They really dug deep into what E&E meant and why it was important to us—and to Victor personally. Maybe I'm wrong about the strange undercurrent. Maybe the urgency just struck me because they spoke frankly about improving sales performance as Victor's top priority.

At one point, I remember, Ron asked where Victor would rank improving E&E among all of Amstand's stated objectives for the year. Victor said something like: "It ties directly into our major corporate goals for revenue and profit growth. Those are Number 1 and Number 2. So E&E is right up there."

Then Ron asked, "To you, personally, where does E&E rank?"
Number 1, Victor said.

I never thought about it from that perspective—which is kind of a
"duh," since I knew our CEO had given E&E to Victor as a major goal.
But I'm not much of a political animal, and I don't sit up nights thinking
about things like, What's the new VP's
biggest hot button?

> *'Their solution
> will be aimed at
> important needs
> that we've
> actually got and
> they actually
> understand.'*

Here's the kicker: GoTeam still hasn't
tried to sell us a solitary thing. That will
happen tomorrow, when Ron and Carrie
come in to present their solution to our E&E
problems. I assume it will be a package of
goods and services. And I'm betting it will be
not only comprehensive, but aimed at
important needs that we've actually got and they actually understand.
That would be a switch from the usual sales presentation.

If it's a great solution, Victor will get to be the genius who found it, I
won't. He's a good guy, and he'll probably give me some credit. I guess
I'm OK with that. If GoTeam's deal allows us to cut back the number of
vendors we use, so I can spend less time listening to a bunch of
pitchmen and more time consulting with Carrie and Ron, I'd be
extremely OK with that.

Conflicted? Yeah. But mainly, I can't believe I'm actually rooting for
a couple of salespeople.

Chapter 2

SHOW ME YOURS AND I'LL SHOW YOU MINE!

Carrie Overton

Salesperson

GoTeam Unlimited

Amstand Companies has a brand new vice president with specific orders to improve efficiency and effectiveness in its sales operation??!! And he hasn't yet figured out what approach to take??!!

When Nancy Winslow dropped that little nugget in our first meeting, I almost jumped out of my skin. Suddenly the Amstand account looked like a whole new ballgame. Dollar signs danced before my eyes. I wanted to grab Nancy by the throat and scream, "Take me to this Victor Herstad character! Now!"

I did no such thing, of course, or anything remotely like it. I can be plenty pushy if need be, but this wasn't the time. For one thing, the

'When you deal with multiple levels of buyers, all of them are important.'

Action Selling system I learned at GoTeam—all right, the system I'm still learning—teaches that when you deal with multiple levels of buyers, all of them are important. Try to bulldoze your way through a mere "influencer" to get to the ultimate decision maker, and you might find out that while the lower-level person can't make the deal, she can sure kill it. I suspected that Nancy might be able to blow me out of the water if she wasn't handled carefully.

So I kept my cool and stayed in what Action Selling calls Act 3,

'The lower-level person can't make the deal, she can sure kill it.'

trying to Ask the Best Questions about what Victor had in mind. *Victor and Nancy*, I reminded myself; must remember to show her respect. But Nancy quickly began to get uncomfortable with my questions about what "efficiency and effectiveness," or E&E, would mean to Amstand.

She doesn't know, I thought. *This is Victor's baby, not hers. Don't embarrass her. Make her an ally. How? I'm not sure.*

'My original Commitment Objective...agreement to meet with me again.'

My original Commitment Objective for the call had been to get Nancy's agreement to meet with me again for a deeper needs analysis of Amstand's current situation. Now I knew about a significant need and that the key contact in the picture was going to be Victor Herstad. Should I ask for a meeting with her and Victor instead? No, I hadn't established a strong enough need for that yet. Help!

That's when I thought of Ron Jensen, GoTeam's sales vice president, my boss and, I suppose, my mentor, though I hate that term. Ordinarily I'd rather break a leg than ask for help, but this account could be a whale. Action Selling talks about the salesperson's role as an orchestrator—one who brings in people and other resources from her company and deploys them intelligently, especially with

> *'The salesperson's role as an orchestrator—one who brings in people and other resources.'*

major accounts. That gives me permission to lean on people like Ron without worrying that they'll think I'm incapable of doing deals myself.

In fact, Ron had told me that he and Darrel—that's Darrel Sharp, GoTeam's CEO—suspected there might be untapped gold in Amstand. I assumed they just meant that my predecessor on the account, Old Marv the Mouth, couldn't uncover an actual customer need with a treasure map and a backhoe. They tried to teach him the Action Selling system— boy, did Ron try—but for the life of him, Marv could not learn to shut his giant blowhole and *listen* to what customers had to say. So finally Ron told him to seek opportunities elsewhere. GabbyLand, maybe. Tragic and all, but geez!

This, however—a new vice president whose whole job was to improve sales E&E, which is basically what GoTeam does—*this* went way beyond the issue of Marv's shortcomings. Not for the first time, I wondered if Darrel was clairvoyant. He has an uncanny sense about these things.

I really need a home run. I need to turn a company like Amstand into a gold mine. My husband works for his father, and the old man pays him peanuts. The idea is that one day my husband will take over the business, and then we'll be on Easy Street. But in the meantime, if I want to keep the health club membership and the cleaning person, I need to bring home the bacon. I don't want a little slice of Amstand's business, sharing the pie with five or six competitors. I want all of it!

At the moment, that meant I wanted an insurance policy. *Bring in Ron.*

Instead of changing my Commitment Objective, I just altered it: Gain Nancy's agreement to meet again for a needs assessment with me—and Ron. Together, he and I would figure out how to get her to agree to put us in a room with Victor.

> ### 'TFBR: Tie Back (to a need you have uncovered), Feature, Benefit, Reaction.'

I did a quick Act 5—Sell the Company—telling Nancy about some clients we had helped, stressing the *range* of solutions that GoTeam offers. She seemed surprised that we could provide anything outside the narrow niche that Marv evidently had liked to yammer about.

Now, how to convince Nancy it would be in her interest to meet with Ron and me? In Act 6—Sell the Product—Action Selling teaches a method called TFBR: Tie Back (to a need you have uncovered), Feature, Benefit, Reaction.

I used the TFBR format, with Ron himself as the "feature" of GoTeam's offering, which was pretty nimble, I thought. It went something like this:

Tie Back: Nancy, it sounds as if Amstand has placed a high priority on improving the efficiency and effectiveness of your sales force.

Feature: GoTeam has an extraordinary vice president named Ron Jensen. He has run six sales organizations that had 100 to 500 salespeople each. I have personally seen him consult with companies that are experiencing challenges very similar to the ones you're describing. (*Not that you're really able to describe much*, I thought.) He is a master at diagnosing these situations and zeroing in on solutions.

Benefit: What that has meant to clients he has worked with is that they were able to put effective solutions into place very quickly and begin to see results almost immediately.

Reaction: How might having access to a specialist like that help you?

It worked! Nancy agreed to meet with Ron and me for a needs analysis. I couldn't wait to tell him.

I rushed back to GoTeam headquarters, caught Ron in a hallway, and gave him the gist. Then he took me to his office, calmed me down, and we replayed the call. That is to say, in Action Selling terms, Ron walked me through an Act 9. I'm still learning the system, as I said. Ron is a grandmaster.

> *'We replayed the call...Ron walked me through an Act 9.'*

I told him what I'd learned about Nancy in Act 2—her history at Amstand, her twin sons, and so on. (By the way, why do people always expect you to find twins fascinating? I mean, two eggs get fertilized, or one divides, or whatever—big whoop. I didn't share this thought with Ron, since he has urged me before to work on my people skills, and of course I didn't share it with Nancy. But seriously, who cares?)

I took him through my Act 3, explaining what my questions had revealed about Amstand and Victor Herstad's new role. "The broad need is to improve sales efficiency and effectiveness," I said. "As for how to do that, they're considering any number of specific needs." Nancy had mentioned several possibilities, as my notes revealed:

Broad Need: Improve sales efficiency and effectiveness

Specific Needs to Investigate:

- Document and follow best sales practices
- Increase new-hire effectiveness
- Fill vacant territories
- Reduce sales cost
- Better sales management info
- More accurate sales forecasts

"We could help them with all of that, Ron," I said excitedly. "We could *own* this account."

Ron looked thoughtful. "You said Nancy told you that Amstand is doing great, right? It owns a quarter of its market, the stock is performing well, and so on?"

"Right," I said.

"So why the sudden concern with boosting sales E&E? Why has this become so important that they turned it into a job for a new vice president? What did Nancy have to say about that?"

> *'Why the sudden concern? Why has this become so important?'*

Damn! That was a question I had missed entirely. I stuck pretty close to the truth in my reply, though. "I didn't want to push her, Ron. She isn't sure what Victor is up to, and she was starting to get embarrassed."

If Ron saw through me, he didn't exactly say so. "That would have been nice to know," he said. "But I agree you were right to back off and regroup when Nancy became uncomfortable."

The main thing, he said, was that I had recognized what kind of opportunity this Victor Herstad guy might represent: "Good job, Carrie."

Ron had only one real criticism for me. In orchestrating large accounts, he said, a basic tactic is to leverage "like titles" to get appointments with people higher up the client's food chain. It works kind of like, "You show me your vice president, I'll show you mine." Instead of bringing my VP, Ron, to the next meeting with Nancy, I should have held him in reserve as a bargaining chip to gain her agreement to let us meet with her VP, Victor. In other words, Ron is an ace in my deck, and I played him too early. Not that we could fix the problem now, of course.

> *'Leverage like titles to get appointments... You show me your vice president, I'll show you mine.'*

I'm sure he's right, in principle. Ron is almost always right. I nodded and agreed, like I was absorbing the lesson. Action Selling does say, "Be an orchestrator – leverage your people resources." I understood that Ron's point was about timing the leverage. But the truth is, I was glad that I did what I did. It meant Ron would be at my side from this moment on. I need to earn some commission. I need to land this account!

We agreed to get together in a few days to devise a strategy for our meeting with Nancy. We already knew what the Commitment Objective would be: Gain her agreement to introduce us to Victor.

In the meantime, though, Ron evidently talked over the Amstand situation with Darrel. Darrel Sharp, remember? GoTeam's CEO. And Darrel—I still can't believe this—Darrel figured out why Amstand was suddenly so worried about improving sales E&E!

Darrel explained it to us as a problem Amstand had with what he called "organic growth." Then Ron explained it to me again in our strategy meeting because, frankly, Darrel understands the workings of public companies *too* well to be great at explaining them to people like me, who are hazy on the mechanics of stockholder meetings and so on.

In a nutshell, here's what happened: Nancy had mentioned that Amstand recently made a couple of acquisitions. Well, Darrel dug up some public reports or documents that revealed (to him) that Amstand's growth was coming not just partly but *almost entirely* from those acquisitions. Its organic growth—meaning its annual revenue increase *without* the new money coming in from the acquisitions—actually lags a few percentage points behind the industry average. In other words, when you look at how well Amstand really is marketing and selling its products, you find it's doing worse that its competitors.

Amstand's financial reports don't show this clearly or directly, it seems, and according to Darrel's research the analysts and shareholders haven't figured it out yet. But they will. When they do, Amstand's stock price could drop like a rock.

"And if the stock takes a big hit, so does Stan Hall," Darrel said, referring to Amstand's CEO. It seems that Darrel knows the guy. They're acquaintances, anyway. "Stan has to be sweating bullets," he said. "This is why he created a new VP and told him to go fix sales efficiency and effectiveness."

Darrel looked at me. "I wonder if your contact Nancy knows about the organic-growth problem," he said. Then he looked at Ron. "I wonder if even Victor knows about it. Amstand wouldn't exactly want to broadcast this news. It wouldn't surprise me if only Stan and probably the CFO really understand what Victor's new job is all about."

Darrel didn't say, "You'll have to be very careful how you use this information with Nancy and Victor." He didn't have to. But now we knew the underlying business issue that made sales E&E an urgent concern—for Amstand Companies, for Stan Hall, and for Victor, though Victor might not be aware of it. We wouldn't need to uncover the client's burning need. We just had to walk though what might be a minefield to bring it out in the open.

By the time Ron and I called on Nancy, we had a well-rehearsed game plan for gaining her agreement to a meeting that included Victor. She really warmed to Ron during Act 2, especially when he pulled those twin nieces out of his hip pocket. (Twins again! And I guess Ron's nieces actually exist. First I've heard of them, thank heavens.)

'Then we'd move on to questions that Nancy probably couldn't answer.'

Act 3 went beautifully. The plan was to use questions that

established the importance of improving sales E&E, but without exposing the organic-growth problem; if Nancy didn't know about it, Victor and Stan would not be happy that *we* spilled the beans. Then we'd move on to questions that Nancy probably couldn't answer, but Victor could. Questions like: How will you know when you have achieved the level of effectiveness you want?

It was vital to do this without making Nancy feel like road kill. Ron was especially good at protecting her ego—never a hint of impatience, never the least sign that he felt we were wasting our time talking to her. But by the time we finished Act 3 and told her a little more about GoTeam and its offerings in Acts 5 and 6, I think several things were clear to Nancy:

One, we were highly professional. Two, we knew a whole lot about their challenges. Three, we sincerely wanted to understand Amstand's needs and to provide solutions that worked; in other words, we could really *help*. And four, to take the process to the next level, Victor had to be in the room.

> ### 'The magic about Action Selling: You sell not by pitching, but by asking questions.'

As Ron and I had planned, I nailed down our opportunity to gain commitment with a modified version of the TFBR I had used in the first call to sell Nancy on the meeting we were having right now. I reminded her about Ron's background, but this time, when I asked for a reaction, I said, "How would having access to a specialist like Ron help Victor in his new responsibility?"

Having gotten a good dose of Ron, she had no qualms at all about presenting him to Victor. Make that presenting *us;* I ain't so bad either. To me, that's the magic about Action Selling. You sell not by pitching, but by asking questions. By Asking the Best Questions in Act 3 – without discussing any specific products or services—we had sold *ourselves* to Nancy. Selling yourself is the salesperson's first and biggest hurdle—and you do it with questions! That insight impresses me more every day.

> **'Selling yourself is the salesperson's first and biggest hurdle—and you do it with questions!'**

Nancy also agreed to pave the way for a phone call from Ron to Victor—a peer-to-peer thing—before the meeting. It was during that phone call that Ron revealed Amstand's organic growth problem to Victor. And yes, it did come as a revelation.

Suffice it to say that tomorrow I will present our formal proposal to the Amstand folks, with Ron along to help answer any questions that come up, and I am *extremely* excited about our chances. Based on our questions, the needs we have helped them clarify, and our confidence that we can meet those needs, they must have a pretty clear notion of the solution we're going to propose. I think they already love it. And we haven't even spelled it out for them yet.

Am I nervous? Sure. I'm not planning to spend my commission until Amstand's check is cashed. But I do believe I'm going to hit my homer.

Chapter 3

MY KINGDOM FOR SOME CLARITY

Victor Herstad

Vice President-Business Development

Amstand Companies

N eedless to say, Ron Jensen impressed me with his first phone call, when it turned out that he knew more about Amstand than I did. At least, he knew more about the underlying problem that explains why I got this job: the little matter of our lagging organic-growth rate, which my CEO, bless his heart, had chosen not to share with me.

But I was even more impressed when I met with Ron. He reminded me of someone. So did his GoTeam sales rep, Carrie Overton, actually. I finally figured out who it was.

About 10 years ago, when I worked for another company, I attended a professional conference that featured a workshop by a highly respected management consultant. The audience was packed with corporate vice presidents and some CEOs from mid-sized firms. I might have been the most junior person in the room. We were at round tables in a big auditorium, eight strangers to a table.

The consultant asked a number of audience members to call out the most pressing "people" issues facing their companies. The responses were predictable: "leadership," "teamwork," "communication," and so on. Then he gave us an exercise: Name your company's most important problem, then explain to the others at your table how you would know an improvement if you saw it.

The way he actually put it was, "What behaviors would you accept as evidence that leadership (or communication, etc.) had improved?"

There were easily 100 people in the room, but I don't think more than five of them succeeded. Nobody at my table did. Even those who had been perfectly confident when naming something like "teamwork" as their No. 1 issue drew an embarrassing blank when they tried to explain what it was, exactly, that they wanted their employees to do differently.

> *'Labeling an issue is one thing; understanding the issue well enough to do something about it is an altogether different matter.'*

The point of the exercise was that labeling an issue is one thing; understanding the issue well enough to *do* something about it is an altogether different matter.

It was that consultant who came to mind as Ron and Carrie questioned me in an Amstand conference room about "sales efficiency and effectiveness." They understood from the start that E&E was just a label. Their questions helped me to think through the things that we actually would have to *do* in order to make meaningful improvements.

I felt as if a fog had lifted. For the three months I'd been in this job, I had been groping to define the right questions, never mind the answers. I walked out of a 90-minute meeting with Ron and Carrie feeling as if I'd made three years' worth of progress.

'Their questions helped me to think through the things that we actually would have to do.'

Yes, I'm talking about a couple of salespeople!

Bless Nancy Winslow, Amstand's sales-support manager, for realizing that the GoTeam folks might be a valuable asset and passing them on to me. If this plays out the way I expect, I'm going to look like a genius. And Nancy knows it. If she were more ambitious—or maybe I should say, if she were a bigger snake—she could have tried to go around me and make this deal her own. That wouldn't have worked, of course, and Amstand would have lost a great opportunity. Nancy did the right thing by the company. I intend to make sure she's recognized for it.

Nancy's enthusiasm for GoTeam had prepared me to expect something more than a run-of-the-mill sales spiel. But what I did not expect when I took the pre-meeting phone call from Ron Jensen was that he would be the one to reveal the true reason for my promotion to this job—the unmentioned problem I had been brought in to solve.

The mystery had nagged at me almost from the start. Naturally, every company would like to maximize the performance of its sales operation. But as far as I knew, Amstand was doing very well. We already own a full quarter of our market, and last year's growth rate of 11 percent beat the industry average of 9 percent. So why was Stan Hall, our CEO, so concerned with improving sales that he created a new vice-president position, complete with associated overhead costs; paid to move me and my family to the headquarters office; and gave me a great big salary bump?

I was delighted with the opportunity, of course. But I was missing something. On the one hand, Stan made it crystal clear that he wanted big-time results from me. My new job was a do-or-die proposition. If I achieved a significant improvement in sales, my future with Amstand was golden. If I failed, I'd be dead meat. Yet I never quite understood the reason behind Stan's urgency. That made me nervous. If it's do-or-die, I kind of like to know what's what.

Then I got the phone call from Ron Jensen. After introducing himself and discussing his proposed agenda for the needs analysis he wanted to conduct with Nancy and me, he dropped his bomb. He did it so gracefully, though, that I'm still not certain if he knew that he was catching me by surprise.

Ron asked if it would be all right for him to pose a question about Amstand's performance. Sure, I said.

"Please correct me if I'm wrong," Ron said, "but I assume that the business issue driving your concern with sales growth is that while your acquisitions are adding significant new revenue, Amstand's organic or real growth rate is lagging behind the industry average. How important is it to turn that situation around?"

Caught off guard, I tried to cover my confusion. I said something like, "I'm not sure our data would support that conclusion." That's when Ron gave me the link to a PowerPoint slide—in the Investor Relations section of Amstand's own web site—that Stan and our CFO had used in a presentation to analysts concerning our last quarterly report. Once I knew what to look for, the seemingly upbeat slide said it all: Yes, Amstand grew by 11 percent last year, but 5 percent of that growth was due to our most recent acquisition. This left us with a real growth rate of only 6 percent—versus the published industry average of 9 percent.

In an instant, everything fell into place. Amstand's value-added sales force is not just our major differentiator from low-cost competitors; it is Stan Hall's own brainchild. He introduced the concept when he got the CEO job 20 years ago, and he has ingrained it into the corporate culture ever since. But our vaunted sales force isn't really responsible for Amstand's impressive 11 percent growth rate. The only thing the salespeople can legitimately claim is the sub-par 6 percent rate of real growth.

I'm surprised that the Wall Street sharks haven't already noticed. Poor Stan must live in terror of the day when they wake up. Because on that day, they will start asking very rude questions about his fundamental strategy. And so will our shareholders.

It wasn't as if Stan had hidden the situation from me. He just didn't call attention to it, for obvious reasons. *I should have realized this on my own*, I thought. After all, the data was in plain sight.

I didn't actually confirm the sales-growth problem for Ron Jensen. I said something to the effect that the picture wasn't necessarily that clear and I would have to look at some of our other numbers. Maybe Ron could tell that the problem came as news to me, or maybe he couldn't. In either case, he behaved as if my discomfort were due simply to the fact that this was sensitive information. He explained that he had not raised the matter in his meeting with Nancy Winslow because he wasn't sure if she was privy to it or if I wished her to be. The implication: He *was* sure that as VP of business development, I was in the loop, and therefore he would not be talking out of school by discussing the issue with me. If he was only trying to spare me embarrassment, he did it very smoothly.

Again without admitting that organic growth did, indeed, seem to represent a ticking bomb for Amstand, I thanked him for recognizing

> ### 'Ron gave me some questions to think about—things that he would like to address in our meeting.'

that the subject was delicate and asked him to keep it off the table in our upcoming meeting with Nancy. Whatever underlying issues might exist, I pointed out, the solution to them was to improve our sales operation.

"Let's focus on that," I said.

Ron agreed, and gave me some questions to think about—things that he and Carrie Overton would like to address in our meeting. They were excellent questions. Given that I naturally would want to measure the impact of any solution I might implement, (*Darn tootin', Ron*, I thought)

> ### 'What levels of improvement would allow us to say that we made a huge difference?'

we would need benchmarks to describe present conditions. So how did I—or Amstand—currently measure sales efficiency and effectiveness? He also urged me to think about measurable goals for improvement—and to think big. "Once we determine the right

metrics," he asked, "what levels of improvement would allow us to say that we made a huge difference?"

At the time, I didn't connect Ron with the consultant who had

> ### 'What is it that we want to accomplish? How will we know success if we see it?'

impressed me so deeply at that long-ago conference, but maybe that's when the memory began to surface. The thrust of his questions was tantalizingly familiar: Let's not waste our time with generic gabble about "maximizing effectiveness." What is it, exactly, that we want to accomplish? And how will we know success if we see it?

A different thought struck me more clearly: *I know you'd like to sell me something, Ron. But you intend to do it by finding a way to turn me into a corporate hero, don't you? You say you'd like me to envision levels of improvement that would let me claim a "huge difference"? My friend, I don't know yet what kinds of goods you can deliver, but you are definitely someone I think I can work with.*

'You are definitely someone I think I can work with.'

That impression was confirmed and strengthened when Nancy and I sat down with Ron and Carrie. Before the meeting, I had done some research of my own that confirmed Amstand's little secret about real growth. To put it bluntly, our value-added sales force wasn't adding enough value to earn its keep.

I had confirmed my new knowledge with CEO Stan Hall, as well. I presented the growth problem to him, PowerPoint slide and all, as something I had discovered on my own—a reason why improving our sales operations was even more vital than I had realized. Stan just nodded. Thankfully, he didn't say, "You've just now figured this out?"

Since the GoTeam people knew our secret and realized that our sales force wasn't pulling its weight, I expected the meeting to include an early question about Amstand's commitment to the value-added sales model. Before analyzing how that model might be improved, Ron and Carrie would need to know whether we intended to junk it altogether and adopt a lower-cost approach. Yet Ron had promised not to reveal the issue to Nancy. I wondered how he would handle it.

He passed my little test with flying colors. Referring only to Amstand's annual report, which speaks glowingly of our value-added sales force and the competitive advantage it brings, Ron asked how important the model is to us as a differentiator. Hugely important, I told him. Our customers love the attentiveness that our salespeople provide, and they appreciate the consistency of having a rep who calls on them routinely. "We are absolutely committed to the value-added model, from the top down," I said.

'Ron and Carrie asked a number of questions that seemed genuinely intended to clarify Amstand's needs.'

To Nancy, this was unremarkable news. But a significant look passed between Ron and me, and I saw that he had received the message. *You and I both know that our sales force isn't cutting the mustard at present. But we're going to rescue it, not put it out of its misery. That idea isn't an option.*

Having established this, Ron and Carrie asked a number of questions that seemed genuinely intended to clarify Amstand's needs, not just to provide excuses for them to try to sell us particular GoTeam products or services. How's that for unusual? I sensed a system at work and a particular philosophy of selling—Ron and Carrie were too well coordinated to be making this up on the fly—but it wasn't any system I knew. A term like "consultative selling" wouldn't begin to do it justice.

Their questions actually helped me think through and clarify the grab bag of needs and concerns that fell under the umbrella heading

'We talked about performance levels, how to measure them, and what would constitute a tremendous boost in results.'

we'd been calling sales E&E— everything from better sales forecasts to getting new hires up to speed faster. We talked in concrete terms about where to find the greatest potential for dramatic improvements. We talked about performance levels, how to measure them, and what would constitute a tremendous boost in results. What would it mean to belt one clear out of the park?

Ron and Carrie asked great questions, listened to the answers, and took careful notes. We were in that conference room for an hour and a half, and I doubt they talked for 15 minutes. When the Q&A was over, they told us just enough about GoTeam to assure me that their company had the capabilities and experience to address the kinds of issues we had discussed.

> *'Ron and Carrie asked great questions, listened to the answers, and took careful notes.'*

A few of Ron's questions had been politely designed to gauge my level of buying authority. He needed to know if he really should be talking to Stan Hall. The same thought had occurred to me after Ron's initial phone call, and I had used my conversation with Stan to clarify—and maybe expand—the scope of my authority.

After establishing that my mission was even more critical than I knew, I told Stan about my upcoming meeting with GoTeam. "I think they may be able to help us with a solution," I said. "What I need to know is this: If I believe that they've got the right answer, how would you like me to involve you in the decision process?"

He took a moment to think about it. Then he agreed to make it my call. If I became convinced that a particular solution was the best way to turn things around in our sales operation, and if the price wasn't insane, Stan would support my decision and back me in case of resistance from the rest of the executive team.

So when Ron Jensen delicately

> *'Rather than a formal presentation, he recommended that we treat it as a working meeting.'*

questioned my buying authority, I essentially told him that he was talking to the right guy. But as we ended our meeting, his suggestion for a next step was surprising for its insight.

Ron proposed that he and Carrie would come back and present to Nancy and me a solution for our challenges. But rather than a final, formal presentation, he recommended that we treat it as a sort of working meeting. Assuming we were basically happy with the proposal, Nancy and I could tweak and refine it. That way we could ensure that the solution addressed all of our own concerns, and also any objections we might anticipate from other Amstand executives.

I found the idea elegant. Ron's subtext, as I read it, was this: Victor, you may be the decision maker in this deal, but you don't need the headaches you'll get if the other power players at Amstand aren't happy about some of the changes involved. So assuming you become convinced that we've got the right solution for you, let us help you sell it to your own people.

'If we've got the right solution for you, let us help you sell it to your own people.'

That proposal meeting—or dress rehearsal, call it what you will—is set for tomorrow. There is already some positive buzz around the company. Yesterday I overheard our IT director—a computer guy, for heaven's sake—telling somebody that, "Stan thinks Victor is close to a deal that will take our sales operation to a whole new level."

Did Stan really say that? I don't know. And obviously I haven't heard GoTeam's actual proposal yet. But unless my instincts are wildly wrong, the sentiment is correct: I think I am just about to light a rocket under Amstand's revenue growth.

Chapter 4

MAKE SELLING A TEAM SPORT

Ron Jensen

Sales Vice President

GoTeam Unlimited

W hen we introduced the Action Selling system at GoTeam two years ago, a lot of attention was placed on the concept of "orchestrating your resources," especially in a complex selling situation. So far, I think our orchestration in the Amstand deal deserves an A.

Maybe I should be a tougher grader and say an A-minus since, tactically speaking, Carrie Overton brought me into play too soon. She could have held me in reserve as a lever she might need to gain Nancy Winslow's agreement to let us meet with her VP, Victor Herstad. Instead, Carrie panicked a little and dragged me in to do the heavy lifting in the earlier meeting with Nancy.

On the other hand, though, maybe it's best that I was there early in the game to backstop Carrie. It was vital to enlist Nancy as an ally who would willingly take us to Victor. At this point in her development, I'm not certain that Carrie could have pulled it off without some direct help from me.

I *am* confident that she's ready right now to manage the Amstand account once it's up and running. Carrie is perfectly capable, though she isn't my favorite employee on a personal level. Sometimes I look at her and see a hammerhead shark. She complains about having to be her household's primary breadwinner because of her husband's family-business deal with his stingy father, but I suspect she enjoys the upper hand she gets in the relationship by out-earning the poor guy. How's that for a creepy thought about someone's marriage?

> *'The whole company is involved in the sales process. Selling has become a team sport.'*

Still, as I say, she's capable. And she's perceptive enough to recognize most of the beauty in the Action Selling system (not all of it yet) and to take advantage of it. That's why she's still here. A few of our other reps aren't.

Whether she presented me to Nancy too soon or not, I'm certainly glad that Carrie *consulted* me as soon as she recognized the potential in the Amstand account. Before we institutionalized Action Selling we expected our reps to act single-handedly: "Go out there and make it rain business." A few of them did just that. But now that Action Selling has given us a common sales language—and everyone speaks it—the whole company is involved in the sales process. Selling has become a team sport at GoTeam. We *talk* to each other about deals. We discuss strategy. We test ideas. Everyone has a common vision about how we'll get the business.

Because Carrie consulted me, I could consult our CEO, Darrel Sharp. Darrel made a huge contribution by penetrating the fog surrounding Amstand's growth rate. When he revealed that the company's expensive sales force actually is underperforming the low-cost competition, we gained a tremendously valuable key to the account.

That key helped open doors all the way to the top of the client's organization. It explained Victor Herstad's new job. And it let us know why Amstand's CEO, Stan Hall, is eager to do whatever it takes to boost sales performance. What's more, it turned out that Darrel knows Stan personally. They're acquaintances rather than close friends—they belong to the same country club—but that gave Darrel enough of an entrée to schedule a phone call with Stan to do some top-level prep work for tomorrow's proposal meeting. Victor Herstad may have the formal authority to buy from us, but nothing on the scale we're shooting for will actually happen at Amstand without Stan's approval.

Did I say tomorrow's proposal meeting? I mean our "working" proposal meeting. I could not be more delighted with that modifier. Nancy and Victor will be acting not only as our advocates but as coaches and guides, helping us craft a solution practically guaranteed to satisfy everyone on Amstand's executive team.

A lot of vendors in our position would have dismissed Nancy, and maybe even Victor, as mere "influencers" and tried to maneuver around them to get to Stan Hall, the ultimate decision-maker. They'd have thought themselves clever for doing it.

> *'Nobody is a mere obstacle...Everybody is a potential ally and coach.'*

Of all the insights contained in the Action Selling system, my favorite might be the one about how to deal with decision influencers in a client company. *Nobody* is a mere obstacle in your headlong charge to get to the person with ultimate buying authority. *Everybody* is a potential ally and coach who can help you navigate through the shoals of a complex sale. The goal is not to maneuver your way around lower-level people as if they were slalom poles on a ski run, with the final buyer at the finish line. The goal is to sell in such a way that those people *want* you to get to the ultimate decision-maker—for their reasons, not yours.

> **'The goal is to sell in such a way that those people want you to get to the ultimate decision-maker.'**

I came up through the sales ranks the hard way, making cold calls on businesses and "doing the numbers" on initial appointments, demos, proposals, and so on. Bitter experience eventually taught me that the advice I kept hearing about how to skip over the heads of lower-level people was deeply flawed. But not until two years ago, when Darrel Sharp passed along an Action Selling book he had found, did I ever see the "everyone's a coach" concept built into a systematic approach to the entire sales process. That's one reason I championed the system at GoTeam.

I've had a lot of sales training in my career. One concept that bugged me about many training programs was their notion of putting

> **'Action Selling teaches that everyone is a decision-maker on something.'**

people in various quadrants based on their personality styles or their authority to buy. There are so many exceptions that I could never agree to the rules. Action Selling teaches that everyone is a decision-maker on *something*. The whole key is that you don't try to sell someone something that they can't possibly agree to buy; but you *do* sell them what they *can* agree to buy. Nancy couldn't agree to buy our solution to Amstand's sales force problems. But she could agree to introduce us to Victor. In fact, she could coach us through the sales process with him.

How do you enlist people as coaches? You get them to buy *YOU*.

And how do you do that? With questions. Asking the best questions earns you the right to ask more questions. Questioning is the true art of selling—and it's the magic of Action Selling. Here's the best part: Everything you need to know about what to ask and how to ask can be learned. Effective questioning is not a talent that you have to be born with. Hallelujah!

'With client advocates coaching you every step of the way, a complex sale isn't nearly so complex.'

Once they've bought *YOU,* every Nancy and every Victor out there can help you plan and fine-tune your entire selling strategy—your next question, your next move, your next commitment objective, your next sales milestone, all of it. With client advocates coaching you every step of the way, a complex sale isn't nearly so complex.

Our sales process for the Amstand deal turned out to be surprisingly similar to our usual format. With Nancy and then Victor acting as our guides, with their own vested interests at stake in our success, the Amstand sales process wound up looking like this:

Sales Process for Amstand

Milestones	Commitment Objectives
1. First Call	Schedule Needs Analysis Meeting
2. Initial Needs Analysis	Agree to Involve Addl. Decision-Makers
3. Phone Call to Addl. D-Makers	Schedule High-Level Needs Analysis
4. High-Level Needs Analysis	Schedule Draft Proposal Meeting
5. Draft Proposal Mtg.	Agree to Recommend Proposal
6. Final Proposal to top Mgmt.	Gain Approval to Implement

As of today, we have completed the first four milestones. The final two milestones have yet to happen. The actual deal should be as good as done after Milestone 5—tomorrow's meeting.

A bit of insurance: This afternoon our CEO, Darrel, will make a phone call to their CEO, Stan Hall. Darrel will assure Stan that his best people are on the project and that he will be reviewing the proposal personally to make sure that it covers all the bases. He'll take Stan's temperature to ensure that he is behind the initiative. If Darrel uncovers any snags that might affect tomorrow's meeting, we'll be prepared to deal with them.

Beginning with Carrie's initial call on Nancy, the driving force behind our whole sales process can be expressed in one word: *Questions.*

> *'When you sell yourself first and customers buy you, everything else about the sales process gets easier.'*

Why does Action Selling work so well? Because it teaches how to sell in a way that matches how customers really buy. When you sell yourself first and customers buy *you,* everything else about the sales process gets easier. Questions are both the roadmap and the vehicle that takes you where you want to go. Asking questions tells you what the customer's issues and preferences are. Questions "open" the sale and create desire for a solution. Questions help you develop your sales strategy. Questions allow you to achieve your commitment objectives. When you ask the best questions and base your actions on the answers, magic happens. People who might have been deal killers enlist in your cause. You find out that those despised "influencers" really do have a lot of influence.

> *'You find out that those despised "influencers" really do have a lot of influence. They use it for you, not against you.'*

And they use it for you, not against you.

Going into my initial phone call to Victor, I didn't know if he was aware of the underlying issue that landed him in his new job. Since it might come as a revelation, and since I didn't want to embarrass him if it did, I decided that the best way to broach the subject was with a question. Though I didn't phrase it quite this way, my question amounted to: "Victor, I see that Amstand's real-growth rate is lagging the industry average. How big a role did that play in the creation of your new position?" That allowed me to throw the organic-growth numbers squarely on the table. And of course I was prepared to show him the documentation on his own web site.

It was pretty obvious from his reaction that Victor hadn't known about it, not that I appeared to notice. So much the better. By revealing it, I not only showed him GoTeam's initiative in researching our clients, I did him a great personal service—the kind of favor a person in his position ordinarily would expect to get from a trusted colleague or consultant, not from a salesperson.

When Carrie and I had prepared for our first meeting with Nancy, we included some questions that she probably couldn't answer. We expected that this would create a need to include Victor in a future meeting. Our commitment objective, after all, had been to gain her agreement to bring Victor into the process.

In my call to Victor, on the other hand, I gave him our agenda for the needs-assessment meeting, including the key questions we'd want to ask. For instance:

1. When you take a critical look at your sales organization and evaluate what they do well and what needs to be improved, what comes to mind?

2. Nancy told us that you're looking for ways to improve the efficiency and effectiveness of your sales force. In order for any solution to demonstrate tangible improvement, there must be a way to measure the current state of affairs. How do you currently measure efficiency and effectiveness?

3. Once we've defined the metrics that will be used to determine current sales performance, and we set goals for improvement... What performance levels will allow us to say that we made a huge difference?

I wanted Victor as well-prepared as possible, because if we intended to craft a great solution for Amstand, we required the best information we could get. By the time I actually met him face to face to begin the meeting, I think he already was about 80 percent sold on me.

'We didn't just want to sell him some products, we wanted to make him a star.'

To go the rest of the distance, Carrie and I had to make it plain that we didn't just want to sell him some products, we wanted to make him a star. How did we do that? With questions. Like Question 3 on my list, several of our queries in the needs analysis meeting were designed to get Victor to visualize what success on a big scale would look like. If we could take him that far, he could fill in the corollary visualization mostly on his own: "How would I feel circling the bases, having hit a grand slam in my company's version of the World Series?"

Victor and Nancy are intelligent people, and we also had to make it clear that we weren't just throwing pixie dust in their eyes. This notion of a big win had to be a vision, not a mirage. We questioned Victor persistently about just what needed to happen for him to get his win, how the implementation would work, and what kinds of metrics we could use to *prove* that his solution—his, not ours—had made a significant difference.

Nailing down those metrics has advantages for GoTeam, as well. Much as we want Victor to feel ownership, in the end it's still our

'What would success look like, and how could he get there?'

solution. Let's just say that if we have the ability to prove, with the client's own numbers, that our answer *works*...well, that kind of helps to keep customers for the long haul. It helps us acquire new customers, too.

By questioning Victor in this manner, we helped him think through his job: What really matters and what doesn't? What would success look like, and how could he get there? Clients tend to appreciate it when you do that. They especially appreciate it when you do it by *asking* them instead of by *pitching* them. That's how we develop strong partnerships with clients; It shows we're on the same team. I'm glad that GoTeam's competitors don't seem to know the secret.

> *'They especially appreciate...asking them instead of pitching them.'*

By the way, GoTeam's growth for the first full year since we adopted the Action Selling system is downright spectacular. And none of it came through acquisitions.

Action Selling teaches that a sale is made or lost before the formal product presentation begins. Amstand is a classic case in point. We've sold ourselves. We've sold our company. And our product? The clients don't yet know the details of the solution we'll propose tomorrow. For that

> *'A sale is made or lost before the formal product presentation begins.'*

matter, we don't know every detail ourselves, since Nancy and Victor will be fine-tuning it with us.

But am I pretty sure that GoTeam is about to land a major new account and that Carrie Overton will get the paycheck of her dreams? You tell me.

Chapter 5

NOW I KNOW A SALES FORCE CAN ADD VALUE!

Stan Hall

CEO

Amstand Companies

I knew Darrel Sharp as someone to say hello to at the Black Bear Yacht Club. I even recalled somebody mentioning that his company, GoTeam, had recently become a much hotter player in its industry. But he's a golfer while my passions are sailing and tennis, so we don't run into each other a lot.

By the time Darrel called to talk about the deal his people are working out with Victor Herstad, I was already thinking I should get to know him better. His company has a way of operating that I want to understand.

I strongly suspect that GoTeam will have the answer to Amstand's sales-performance problem. That is an enormous relief to me. But it's almost a greater relief to know for sure that there *is* an answer out there—I mean, regardless of what happens with GoTeam. Now I'm certain that a value-added sales force not only should be but *can* be a terrific differentiator and the foundation of a winning strategy, even in the Age of the Internet.

I'm watching that kind of differentiation unfold in real time, as GoTeam's own value-added salespeople pursue our business. I see the proof every time I look into Victor's face and behold a newly energized executive who is filled with confidence—contagious confidence—that he's going to turn this ship around.

'The magic has to lie in the way they sell and the value they add in the course of selling.'

Victor's new attitude doesn't come from any pitch GoTeam made for a particular product or service—a better mousetrap or a magic lamp with a genie inside. Evidently they haven't actually pitched anything at all yet. That means the magic has to lie in the way they sell and the value they add in the course of selling.

In other words, their salespeople do exactly what our sales force is supposed to do. They do what I have always believed a great sales force *could* do. They add value. That's why I have kept Amstand on the value-added path for 20 years, ever since I became CEO.

About a year ago I began to doubt myself. Believe me, self-doubt is not something I'm used to. I built Amstand into the No. 1 company in its industry. No brag, just fact. On a tennis court I can beat the pants off players half my age. Want to know why the Black Bear Yacht Club sponsors nationally known sailing regattas? Because I organized them and put Black Bear on the map, that's why.

But for many months a small voice had whispered depressing thoughts. Maybe I had become a dinosaur, unable to see new realities or adapt to a new environment. Like many industries, ours has been turning into a straight commodity business, with customers buying on price alone. Most of our competitors now take the low-cost commodity route, using the Internet as their primary selling vehicle, with skeleton crews of salespeople as backup.

I have fought the trend for all I'm worth. I can't count the number of times I have insisted to

> **'60 to 80 percent of potential customers are really value buyers.'**

our shareholders that selling on price is a trap, that we don't want pure price buyers as customers anyway, that 60 to 80 percent of potential customers are really *value* buyers, waiting only for someone to explain the extra value that exists in our services and why it is worth a little more money. (Come to think of it, based on what Victor has said about GoTeam's determination to understand our needs on a deep level, I wonder if our salespeople do too much explaining and not enough listening?)

At any rate, last year the tide of change finally seemed to overtake my philosophy. If you leave our latest acquisition out of the picture, Amstand's growth rate fell below the industry average. In real terms, head to head, our low-cost competitors are outperforming us.

I'm glad that Victor uncovered our little growth secret; in my mind that was a test for him, and now he has passed. But Wall Street analysts are a different story. When they look harder at the numbers and realize that I have been championing a strategy based on a value-added sales force that isn't adding value, "dinosaur" is the kindest thing they'll call me.

I am 68 years old. I intend to retire at 70, even though retirement looks boring to me. What do retired people do? I love sailing and tennis, but not as full-time occupations.

For a while, though, I actually thought about pulling the plug early. Just announce that I was leaving to pursue other interests and walk away. Why did I have to keep on proving myself to the world anyhow? Hadn't I proved enough?

One factor, I confess, was the thought that the stock options I would exercise at retirement would be worth considerably more before the analysts figured out Amstand's problem with real growth and proceeded to hammer its stock like vandals busting up a china shop. I can't say I'm too fine a person for that consideration to occur to me, and I wouldn't believe anyone who told me he was.

But I'm not exactly desperate where money is concerned. My net worth is in the high eight figures, and it will stay in that range regardless of my options' value. The little voice telling me to step down had more to do with a loss of confidence. Maybe the world really had passed me by. My core belief about the way Amstand should do business no longer seemed to hold water. I didn't know how to fix the problem. Maybe the company would be better off without me.

Self-pity is even more foreign to me than self-doubt, however. I'd be damned if I would run away like a rat and leave behind a mess for someone else to clean up. If I couldn't figure out how to invigorate our sales performance and jump-start our real growth rate, maybe someone else could. I reached into our most successful branch office and tapped Victor Herstad.

I brought Victor to headquarters, gave him a VP title, and handed him a single assignment: boost the efficiency and effectiveness of our sales organization. How? That was for him to determine. I told him the field was wide open and that I didn't want him to start with any preconceived ideas. I let him know that if he succeeds, the sky is the limit for him at Amstand. If he fails, he'll be out on his can.

My stake in the game? My reputation and my legacy rest on the value-added model I created 20 years ago and have nurtured ever since. Victor's success would be my success—and my vindication.

That much he knows. Here is what he doesn't know about the decision I made when I chose to stick it out as CEO for two more years: If the value-added model could not be rescued and Amstand had to join the ranks of price sellers, I would make that call myself. Before I stepped down at 70, I would at least start the process of dismantling our sales force and changing the company's strategic direction.

My legacy still would be in tatters. Everyone would say I waited too long to bow to the inevitable. But nobody would be able to say I had run away from the death of my cherished vision. If it had to be buried, I would bury it with my own hands.

I hoped desperately that it wouldn't come to that, of course. I gave Victor all the support I could. But I couldn't give him the answer because I didn't *know* the answer. Worse, I was afraid there might be no answer.

Then Victor found GoTeam. Or rather, he tells me, our sales-support manager, Nancy Winslow, found them. I don't care. What matters is that all of a sudden, Victor stopped acting like a guy who was trying to find the right door and started behaving like someone with his hand wrapped around the handle.

His whole demeanor has changed. He talks about the various elements of our sales organization much more clearly and precisely. He seems able to visualize what has to happen and why—which of our needs are most pressing and where the greatest leverage can be found. Even his questions have become more penetrating. He's no longer just thinking about how to boost our growth rate but about how we should track and measure the improvements we're going to achieve. Not *might* achieve, mind you; the improvements we're *going* to make.

He has been discussing all this not only with me but with other people in the company. And like I said, his new confidence is contagious. Our chief financial officer is one of the few people who thoroughly understand the nature and implications of our dilemma with organic growth. Two days ago the CFO popped into my office grinning. "Just had an interesting conversation with Victor," she said. "I only saw the general shape of where he's going, but he has cracked it, hasn't he, Stan? He's got a plan to save our bacon. What is it that you haven't told me?"

"I'm not sure of the details yet myself," I replied, grinning back. "But yes, I think our boy is definitely onto something."

Victor is still hedging his bets, of course. He points out to me that he has committed us to nothing. He says he will not recommend a proposal from GoTeam unless he's completely satisfied that it is realistic, doable, and will produce significant, measurable improvements. He will go over their proposal himself until he is either sure that it is the best deal for us or he determines that they don't have the right solution after all.

'You really think these people have all the right answers, don't you?'

Not much chance of that, Victor, I thought. *I've never seen anyone as sold on a company as you are on GoTeam.*

"You really think these people have all the right answers, don't you," I asked, challenging him a little. He didn't get defensive. He just smiled, as if at a private joke. "It's more like they have all the right questions," he said. "If this works out the way I think it will, remind me later to tell you about a conference speaker I heard a long time ago."

> *'It's more like they have all the right questions.'*

I'm guessing that this will, indeed, work out as Victor expects, and that our sales organization will get the boost it needs. At least I'm awfully hopeful. It's been too long since I felt hopeful.

Am I worried that Victor is *too* sold on GoTeam? On the contrary. Maybe the best part of this, as far as I'm concerned, is the proof that value-added salespeople really *can* turn potential customers into trusting allies and supporters. I respect Victor's abilities; if I didn't I wouldn't have put him in this job. If GoTeam can win his loyalty, and even make him a determined advocate,

> *'Value-added salespeople really can turn potential customers into trusting allies and supporters.'*

then our salespeople should be able to do the same with our clients.

This deal is barreling forward like a freight train, straight toward a solution that will put Amstand into a close partnership with GoTeam. So I've already got proof that my faith in the value-added model is justified, Internet or no Internet. We obviously haven't been executing it well enough, but the concept works!

By selling Victor so well, GoTeam had pretty much sold me before I got the phone call from Darrel Sharp. The call was just icing on the cake, though I appreciated the personal touch from their CEO. We chatted a little about Black Bear. He asked what I had heard so far about the work that GoTeam hoped to do for Amstand. He told me that his VP, Ron Jensen, and salesperson Carrie Overton were two of his very best people. He assured me that he would monitor things personally to make sure that we got both the right solution for our needs and the follow-up service necessary to implement it. We agreed to talk again once a formal proposal is on the table.

Darrel doesn't know the half of it. I'll talk to him again, all right. And then I'll track him down, at the club or somewhere else, and pick his brain about the way *his* sales organization works. Somehow he has captured lightning in a bottle. I want it.

Chapter 6

I Found a Secret Weapon

Darrel Sharp

CEO

Go Team Unlimited

"It's moving like a freight train." That was Stan Hall's first laughing response when I asked what he knew about the deal our people are working on with his man Victor Herstad.

In part, Stan was flexing a little muscle, letting me know that he wasn't going to be run over, and he could derail us if he chose. But there was more admiration in his voice than warning. He was impressed.

I know just what you mean, my friend, I thought. *That's what Commitment Objectives bring to the table. You'd be amazed how many of our deals gain momentum like this since we adopted Action Selling.*

The Commitment Objective concept was the first thing that really leaped out at me when I happened to pick up the book, "Action Selling: How to Sell Like a Professional Even If You Think You are One." That was almost two years ago now. It was the first step on a journey that has completely transformed our business.

> *'Action Selling insists that you always have a Commitment Objective for sales calls.'*

Action Selling insists that you *always* must have a Commitment Objective for sales calls. This is a predetermined goal to gain the customer's agreement to take the next logical step that will move the sales process forward: Gain Nancy Winslow's agreement to bring Victor into the process. Gain Victor's agreement for a working proposal meeting. The ball never stops rolling. The momentum never stops building.

My phone call to Stan had a Commitment Objective: to gain his agreement that he and I would talk again after GoTeam's proposal was presented. I had additional goals, of course. During the call I wanted to reassure him that GoTeam was the right choice and that I, as CEO, would make it my personal business to see that our solution meets all of

> *'Commitment Objective forces our salespeople to identify what that next step should be and then ask the customer to take it.'*

Amstand's needs. I described Ron and Carrie as my best people and pointed out that his team, Victor and Nancy, has forged a great relationship with my team. But above all, I succeeded in gaining Stan's commitment to take that next step.

There always must be a next step. Always. No matter how complex the sale, or how winding the path to reach the moment when the ultimate authority makes a final buying decision, having a Commitment Objective for every call forces our salespeople (and me) to identify what that next step should be and then ask the customer to take it. Our rule: "No Commitment Objective, no sales call."

When I first encountered the concept, I thought of Woody Allen's line in "Annie Hall" about how a relationship is like a shark: It has to keep moving forward or it dies. Then and there the idea struck me that if GoTeam institutionalized Cómmitment Objective as a requirement for every salesperson on every call, we would have a built-in mechanism to ensure that our client relationships kept moving forward.

I still picture a shark, but if the momentum made Stan think of a freight train, that was fine. His metaphor actually may be better because it suggests a machine with a lot of moving parts. It isn't the Commitment Objective concept alone that moves our deals ahead but the fact that it is built into a systematic process. The elements in that process work together to make it far more likely that customers will, in fact, agree to take that next step.

Action Selling's emphasis on questioning skills is key. Great questions do a lot for a sale, but above all they build trust. No matter how good the pitch, a customer who has been *pitched* has no reason to trust a salesperson enough to keep on taking those steps. But a customer

> *'A customer who has been expertly questioned has every reason to believe that the salesperson cares about him.'*

who has been expertly *questioned*—and listened to, and understood— has every reason to believe that the salesperson cares about him and his real needs. *Of course* a customer will walk hand in hand toward a solution with a partner who has earned his trust and obviously is dedicated to finding the best solution. I would. So would you.

In an average one-hour sales call, our top reps now spend about 50 minutes in what Action Selling calls Acts 2, 3, and 4: building personal rapport, asking the best questions, and checking their understanding of the customer's needs until they're sure they've reached agreement on what those needs are. That's where the real selling takes place. Our people spend maybe 10 minutes of that hour "selling" GoTeam and its products.

That is a 180-degree reversal of the way most salespeople handle a sales call. It's a complete reversal of the way our own sales reps used to operate.

It was a great day for GoTeam when I found that book. I'm glad I didn't have to push and prod Ron Jensen to turn Action Selling into our standard business process. He came up through the sales ranks, like I did. He'd seen a lot of training programs, like I had. Once he got a look at Action Selling, he ran with it. All I had to do was let everyone know I was onboard with the idea, then stay out of Ron's way.

I'm happy I was able to help him out with the Amstand account by uncovering Stan Hall's problem with organic growth. I knew that *something* was peculiar as soon as Ron told me what Carrie Overton had learned on her initial call. Stan isn't the kind of CEO who hands out VP titles like Halloween candy. Why would he suddenly create a position for a new "vice president of business development" whose sole job actually was to shake up the sales organization?

I called my stockbroker and asked for some research on Amstand. One of the things he sent back was a link to an audio recording of the company's last quarterly investors' meeting. It was in the Investor Relations section of Amstand's web site. I listened to Stan Hall reiterate his commitment to a value-added sales strategy and vow to instill it in the new division created by Amstand's latest acquisition.

I began to sift though the financial reports that were distributed at the meeting. Sure enough, hiding in plain sight on a PowerPoint slide, there was the smoking gun: Take away the acquisition, and Amstand's real growth rate was pathetic compared with its industry's average.

Stan's sales strategy wasn't working. Hence, Victor Herstad's new job.

When I laid it out for Ron and Carrie, he understood the implications immediately. She got the gist but tried unsuccessfully to hide her confusion about what, exactly, the numbers meant. I stressed to both of them that when an account is a public company, it is always worthwhile to sniff around in the Investor Relations section of its web site. You won't often find something as dramatic as I did in this case, but you will always learn things that point toward avenues to explore when you prepare questions for a sales call.

> *'When an account is a public company, sniff around in the Investor Relations section of its web site.'*

I'm afraid that advice won't be much use to Carrie unless we educate her somehow on the workings of corporate finance. Maybe we should do that with our other salespeople, too. Invest in a course on "business literacy"? It's something to think about.

As for Ron, I believe he was disappointed with himself that he hadn't beaten me to it. Next time, he might. I have more grounding in finance than he does, but he is perfectly capable of extracting meaning from a company's numbers.

If I'm better than Ron at this kind of investigation, I suppose the reason is that he went straight into sales on purpose while I got there by accident. I graduated with a business degree. I actually thought I'd be hired as an executive right out of college. I took my first sales job as a fallback option, feeling unappreciated by dimwitted executive recruiters. But the experience transformed me. I found I was good at sales, and I loved the excitement of winning business. I never looked back. Eventually I became a sales manager, then came to GoTeam as VP-sales, then president, and finally CEO.

I couldn't begin to count the number of sales books I've read or seminars I've attended over the years. My first two employers put their salespeople though so many flavor-of-the-month programs that nobody knew what the heck to do from one day to the next. I picked up some helpful ideas here and there, but finally I came around to the point of view that great salespeople are probably born, not made. I quit expecting to find a systematic program that relied on *learnable* skills to drive the entire sales process in a predictable direction.

So Action Selling came as a wonderful surprise. It relies entirely on skills and techniques that really can be taught, from "relationship skills," to questioning, to handling objections and gaining commitment. So far, the only people I have found who can't learn the system are a few veteran pitchmen whose bad habits are too deeply ingrained to *unlearn*.

'The system has formalized our call-planning process... It has formalized our sales management process.'

The system has formalized our call-planning process so that we pay far more attention to developing the best questions to ask. It has formalized our sales management process by pushing us to think in terms of specific milestones for every account. Our salespeople always know where they are with a client and where they're headed, just as Ron and Carrie know that tomorrow's milestone is a working proposal meeting with the Amstand people, and that it has a high probability of success. That makes revenue forecasting a whole lot easier.

We even speak a new language at GoTeam. Business jargon has a bad reputation, deservedly, because it so often disguises meaning instead of clarifying it. But good professional jargon is a form of shorthand that allows insiders to communicate complex information quickly and precisely. Two auto mechanics can have a more productive conversation about a "U-joint" than about "that half-circle doohickey underneath the car."

Action Selling brings with it a precise vocabulary that makes everything about the sales process far easier to judge, coach, and discuss. Since we make sure that

> **'A precise vocabulary makes everything about the sales process far easier to judge, coach, and discuss.'**

everyone at GoTeam is trained on the system, even the customer-support people talk in terms of Commitment Objective, Agree on Need, Company Story, and so on. When Ron or I tell a salesperson to walk us through an Act 9, the rep knows we want a thorough debriefing on a call, with an emphasis on areas to improve upon in future calls.

I have always believed that effective communication is a key to success in any business. We never had a precise, efficient language to speak when it came to sales. Now we do. Our conversations are as clear as the skyrocketing trend lines in GoTeam's revenues and market share since we began to master the Action Selling system.

We also talk *more often* with each other about what's happening with accounts. It has to do with leveraging our people resources. Two years ago, Carrie Overton might not have gone straight to Ron with the news about Amstand's new vice president, and Ron might not have discussed it with me. I never would have found the problem with real growth that provided him with such a powerful lever.

> **'Our new sales language is a model for the effective communication that we seek to establish with customers.'**

I think of our new sales language as a kind of model for the effective communication we seek to establish with customers. After all, what is the real purpose of a sales call in which the rep spends 90 percent of the time asking questions, listening to the answers, and checking understanding? Here's my answer: The purpose is

'Crystal-clear communication: That's what enables trust.'

to achieve crystal-clear communication. That's what enables trust. It happens only when the salesperson learns enough to understand the customer's situation, the business challenges behind it, and the personal needs that drive it.

More than anything, that's what Ron and Carrie did at Amstand. They clarified the business challenge and kept digging until they understood how it personally impacted all of the players—Stan, Victor, and Nancy. That's why this deal started with Nancy's reluctant meeting

'They kept digging until they understood how it personally impacted all of the players.'

with an unfamiliar salesperson and progressed to the point where Nancy and Victor are acting as GoTeam's coaches, guides, and champions. In a complex selling environment, the competitor who achieves that understanding best...wins.

Speaking of GoTeam's competitors, they're naturally curious about how we've been winning so much business lately—including business they thought was theirs. At an industry conference last month, no fewer than six

'The competitor who achieves that understanding best...wins.'

of them tried to pump me about the secret behind our recent surge.

I told them we've just been on a hot streak. "I'm only worried that our luck will even out eventually," I said. The longer they think that, the better. Because things aren't going to even out. Not unless they discover Action Selling. And I sure won't be the one to tell them.

ORDER MORE BOOKS!

TO ORDER BOOKS:

- Call (800) 232-3485
- www.ActionSelling.com
- Fax (763) 473-0109
- Mail to The Sales Board

$19.95	Retail
3.00	Discount
$16.95	Reader Price

QUANTITY	BOOK	BOOK ORDER FORM
☐	Action Selling	
☐	Selling Your Price	**SHIPPING AND HANDLING**
☐	Questions: The Answer to Sales	$4.95 per US order
☐	Masters of Loyalty	Can/Int'l actual cost
☐	Sales Strategy From The Inside Out	Payable in US funds

BILL MY CREDIT CARD

THE SALES BOARD
14505 21ST AVE. N.
PLYMOUTH, MN 55447

Card# _____ Exp. _____

DISC _____ VISA _____ MC _____ AMEX _____

Signature _____

Bill to _____	# of Books _____
Address _____	Price $ 16.95
City _____ ST ___ Zip _____	Total $_____
Daytime phone _____	MN Sales Tax $_____
Ship to _____	Ship/Handling $ 4.95
Address _____	Total Due $_____
City _____ ST ___ Zip _____	

Please allow 5-7 days for US Delivery. Can/Int'l orders please allow 10 days.
This offer is subject to change without notice

Get Trained and Certified as an *Action Selling* Professional!

Want to learn more about how Action Selling can help your organization realize its full sales potential? For information about training and certification for yourself or your salespeople, contact The Sales Board.

Founded in 1990, The Sales Board has boosted the performance of more than 2,500 companies and 300,000 salespeople worldwide in virtually every industry. Action Selling provides a systematic approach to managing and conducting the entire sales process. Our complete training program provides all the necessary tools for students and instructors. Training is customized specifically for each organization's selling situation and even for individual salespeople.

Studies document that veteran salespeople who become Action Selling Certified improve their sales performance by an annual average of 16 percent. As for rookie salespeople, there is no finer system to start them off on the right foot and make them productive immediately.

Students participate in a highly interactive two-day training session facilitated by our talented trainers or by their own Action Selling Certified managers. Students then take part in Skill Drills to refine and reinforce their new skills in the field. Accountability is built into the process with management reinforcement, plus an assessment and certification system.

To learn more about the complete Action Selling training and certification system, please contact us or visit our Web site:

The Sales Board
(800) 232-3485
www.TheSalesBoard.com
www.ActionSelling.com

ABOUT THE AUTHOR

Duane Sparks is chairman and founder of The Sales Board, a Minneapolis-based company that has trained and certified more than 300,000 salespeople in the system and the skills of Action Selling. He is the author of four Best Selling books; *Action Selling, How to sell like a professional even if you think you are one; Selling Your Price, How to escape the race to the bargain basement; Questions: The Answer to Sales; and Masters of Loyalty, How to Turn your Sales Force into a Loyalty Force.*

In a 30-year career as a salesperson and sales manager, Duane has sold products ranging from office equipment to insurance. He was the top salesperson at every company he ever worked for. He developed Action Selling while owner of one of the largest computer marketers in the United States. Even in the roaring computer business of the 1980s, his company grew six times faster than the industry norm, differentiating itself not by the products it offered but by the way it sold them. Duane founded The Sales Board in 1990 to teach the skills of Action Selling to others.